Hold on to
what is good
and nurturing to
the end ❤️

MOTHERLESS

MOTHERLESS:
MEMOIRS OF A TEENAGE GIRL

CARSEN AMINNA

MOTHERLESS:
MEMOIRS OF A TEENAGE GIRL

iUniverse books may be ordered through booksellers or by contacting:

iUniverse
1663 Liberty Drive
Bloomington, IN 47403
www.iuniverse.com
1-800-Authors (1-800-288-4677)

Because of the dynamic nature of the Internet, any web addresses or links contained in this book may have changed since publication and may no longer be valid. The views expressed in this work are solely those of the author and do not necessarily reflect the views of the publisher, and the publisher hereby disclaims any responsibility for them.

Any people depicted in stock imagery provided by Getty Images are models, and such images are being used for illustrative purposes only.
Certain stock imagery © Getty Images.

ISBN: 978-1-5320-6635-1 (sc)
ISBN: 978-1-5320-6640-5 (hc)
ISBN: 978-1-5320-6636-8 (e)

Print information available on the last page.

iUniverse rev. date: 01/16/2019

Letter to my teen self...

Hey Girl,

I know things really appear to suck right now, but they get greater later. And while you may feel abandoned, God has not left your side. Everyone is not going to understand you, and it's not your job to make them. Some folks just don't want to see things any other way but their own. Also, not being included is often times a blessing in disguise-don't try to fit a square peg in a round hole.

Remember, love does not hurt, and there is nothing cute about jealousy on your end or in your significant others. When people show you who they are, please, by all means, believe them! You are incredibly perfect with all your imperfections, because you have been made in the image and likeness of God, and if you give yourself enough time, your rough edges will be made smooth through life experiences, His grace, and His mercy.

Be patient with yourself. People come and people go consider yourself blessed to have one good friend that is there through it all. Surround yourself with people that have your best interest at heart and use wisdom liberally. Tell people exactly how they've made you feel, and make no apologies for it. Protect your heart and always seek God first.

In closing, love every part of you...even the most difficult pieces, those are the parts that if nurtured, will push you into your greatness.

With Love & Much Hope for the Future

Acknowledgements

Thank you to my beautiful mother, truly you have left your mark upon this world, and it continues to resonate through me. I am most proud to have been your daughter and honored that God chose me. Your prayers, strength, and love exceed all space and time, and I will forever carry you in my heart, for they are the very things that have carried me.

To my father, you always said you were proud of me, and it was reflected in the way you talked about me to everyone you encountered. To know you, was to love you! I proceed every action that I take with that warm thought leading the way.

Thank you to everyone that has had a part in my life, past and present, whether good, bad, or indifferent, know that every interaction has helped to mold me into the beautifully flawed, courageous, God-seeking woman I am today.

Special thanks to my husband, who is an army without numbers all by himself; I could not have done this without you encouraging me to speak my truth. Your love and patience has assisted in smoothing those rough edges, that most will never understand.

To my four beautiful blessings, Anniah, Amir, Carter & Saundra...I thank God for each one of you! What you read here is very much a part of who I am and what has made me the mother that you are learning to love, as I am you.

It matters not the amount of time we spent,
though it be short, you penetrated my soul,
you left and I can still feel your presence—
and for me, that is all that truly matters.

-Carsen Aminna

1

A SHIFT IN THE ATMOSPHERE

My mother died in the wee hours of the morning on April 29, 1996, in the comfort of her home in her bed. I was a fresh fifteen years young and still trying to figure myself out and also the world around me. I was not very impressionable, unlike most teens my age, and more often than not, walked to the beat of my own drum, even if it resulted in an error. That morning, while sitting on the floor of my mother's living room, knees bent under me at my sister, Leah's feet, who was sitting on the couch; I realized nothing would ever be the same. I had been catapulted into a world that I never dreamed I would be a part of, at least not that early in life. A world where a mother's love could never be tangible again; the protection of her strong arms could never be felt again; the selfless, undeniable giving of herself without conditions could never be experienced again. Not really feeling anything but exhaustion and an emptiness that continued to gnaw at me, I sat and listened to my sister be comforted by her husband, Ryan. I remember him asking us "how we felt," and we both replied, "Numb." The shock that my mama, my "forever girl," was gone and wasn't coming back, was too much to bear. I remember feeling all alone, despite having a sister, really close friends, and other family. I felt that no one could understand what I was experiencing, and for the most part, that was true.

The first person I called was my best friend. She was the very first person I met when my family moved to the neighborhood in 1987, and we had, what I believed at the time, was a close friendship. Despite us attending two different schools, most of our childhood we had a bond. She and her family knew my mother had been battling with breast cancer, and it was nearing the end. With tears in my eyes and despair in my throat, I called to receive comfort. Comfort that I did not find. While she offered the cliché statement of "I am sorry for your loss," I felt she made no real concerted effort to be there for me. In my heart, I wanted more from her as my friend. I wanted her to come over and just sit with me, even if she didn't have the words. Her presence would have been enough. Hanging up the phone with her in those early morning hours, I soon discovered what would become a consistent pattern with not just her failing me as a friend, but others as well.

My mother was by all intents and purposes a "people person." She loved immensely hard those she cared for, and it showed in her actions and words. She was also very strong. I'd like to think... in fact... I know, I inherited that from her. Her wit, strength, sense of humor, and no-nonsense attitude is what attracted most people to her. All of these, I possess as well, but her strength, which was strongly rooted in Jesus Christ, is the thing I am the proudest of and the thing that I believe has gotten me through many obstacles in life.

The remainder of that morning is still a mystery to me. I do not remember if we chose to stay at the house or go to my sister's house. I do remember not going to school the very next day; however, I do know that I went later on in the week. I guess you can say we were prepared for her death; her battle with cancer was fought over the course of a year and a half, and when her last breath came and went, there was a wave of relief that washed over us because she was finally at peace and without pain.

I had roughly about six weeks of school remaining and getting transferred was not something that made sense. I was a student-athlete and ran track for my high school. I wanted to remain committed to the team, and also had no desire to be uprooted any further than I already had been, so staying and finishing up only seemed right. Upon my return to school the same week of my mother's death, surprisingly, everyone knew. I only had really one person that I considered a true friend there, and I can't imagine that she told everyone; however, every class period, every passing period was jammed packed with sorrowful glances, whispering of teachers, and students alike, offering their condolences. It was absolutely, positively too much. I am an introvert's introvert; no doubt about it, so to be overcome with so much attention was nauseating. In addition to me being an introvert, at the time, I had a very black and white way of thinking. Perhaps it was developmental and all a part of coming into who I was and who others were to me, but I had a very defined line of who my friends, associates, and enemies were. These lines were developed over the course of fifteen years with having been bullied by some, tolerated by others, and accepted by very few.

Having known enemies come to me to offer condolences was foreign to me; it outraged me and quite honestly, boiled my blood. However, while I steamed and stewed on the inside, my actions were more muted on the outside. I showed my distaste for their offering of condolences by making biting comments and remarks that were clearly stamped" return to sender," and that was not well received. In fact, one interaction resulted in myself and another girl (a teammate) and her sister being sent to the school counselor. The girl actually attempted to hurl a chair at me! Angered because I questioned the reason for her speaking to me, even at a time like this-especially at a time like this, she spewed hateful and nasty insults at me in front of the school counselor, who was completely appalled. My teammate's actions and words were hurtful and spoke volumes as to why I didn't want her fake condolences or concerns to begin with. I was absolutely and completely numb. As I recall, I caught the bus home that day, and feeling depleted and overwhelmed, I rode home in silence.

The next day, I attended track practice and successfully ignored the girl I had the altercation with the previous day. Unfortunately, we both ran track and our sport's lockers were in the same section, and there was no avoiding each other, but I could definitely play deaf and dumb. The practice had gone reasonably well and was nearing the end when another teammate by the name of Kelly, approached me. She was a known bully in the school and often times had said mean things to me in the past. When she asked, was I okay and was something wrong, I elected to tell her I was good. I could sense that she was more persistent in knowing the ins and the outs of my mother's death, than truly being concerned about my welfare. The only time she had spoken to me in the past was to make fun of me. As a result of not getting the answers she sought, she lashed out at my response. A barrage of words flew from her mouth, aiming to insult and embarrass me, along with her physically attempting to do harm to me on the track field because I rejected her "concern." Thankfully, my friend intervened and told Kelly to leave me alone.

As I dismissed myself from the field that afternoon, I was filled with irritation and frustration, anger and of course, hurt. To my surprise, my uncle, my mother's brother was waiting for me in the parking lot. This was not my normal routine, and I had not asked for his presence, but I was thankful. I was thankful for the quiet, air-conditioned ride home free from unapologetically loud and rude kids with questions and "concerns." I was thankful for the shift in the atmosphere.

Most situations that occurred shortly after my mother's death are a blur. Connecting the dots on how certain events took place are either crystal-clear or very, very fuzzy. During those last weeks of school, I still returned home after practice, and slowly, the furniture began being moved out. The couch, the television, the coffee table, and a host of other things were gone. My bedroom furniture remained until I left-then it disappeared. The house suddenly became eerie to me. The home, which I had lived in since the age of five, was now unfamiliar and cold, distant, and downright scary.

I continued to be in my childhood home and returned there every day after track practice. At home, I would wash clothes and complete homework. Once I was done for the day, I would walk about three blocks to my mother's best friend's house. Leah and I affectionately called her, Aunt Sandy. Aunt Sandy lived alone at the time and never had children, so her house was just what I needed. She didn't bother me at all, and she wasn't pushy to make me talk. However, on one occasion, she informed my sister that I was coming over, going straight to the room that she allowed me sleep in, and was closing the door. My sister, being the extrovert that she is, chastised me about coming into someone's house and shutting myself off to them. She hadn't taken into consideration my feelings, my thoughts, or my position. I don't even think it bothered my Aunt Sandy; honestly, she was probably more concerned than anything. I remember feeling invalidated by my sister's comments; this was an all too familiar feeling. In most of the situations involving my mother's sickness and death, I felt that way because I was treated that way. During that time, I was never let in on dynamics of the circumstances, always receiving bits and pieces of information but never the full story.

You can basically say Leah and I were each raised like "the only child." We are twelve years apart in age, and our experiences are surprisingly sometimes completely different as it pertained to our rearing. However, she still assumed the position as the older sister and treated me accordingly. In fact, everyone in our family treated me like the baby. Most situations centered around my mother's sickness were kept from me. Doctor's visits, diagnosis, prognosis, treatments - you name it; it was all done with a touch of secrecy. I had no clue, until the very end, just how sick my mother actually was, and that she was experiencing all the pain and suffering she had. I was kept in the dark. I believe that most of the family's directives in terms of keeping me "protected" came from my mother. While hindsight is 20/20, and I understand now fully why she chose to keep some things away from me, I still, to this day, would have preferred to know the extent of things. When we know better, we do better. And, while I have no regrets in the way that I treated her because I treated her good regardless,

I would have wanted to spend more intimate time talking with her, sharing with her...loving on her. I would have made different choices in terms of hanging with friends and attending certain outings. I guess these are things that my mother did not want me to have to choose between, but it was my choice and my decision, and it was stripped from me. Children are a lot more resilient and understanding to sensitive subject matters than adults give them credit for. I would have gladly forgone some events in my life, for one more moment with her. Even now.

The stain of rejection is only
as lasting as we desire…

-Carsen Aminna

2

SUMMER OF '96

The summer began, and I officially moved out of my childhood home. I was roughly twenty minutes or about eleven miles away from everything and everyone I held dear to me; while it was nothing but a short distance, it felt like two very different worlds. The separation felt like I was being punished for a crime I didn't commit. Soon after moving in with my pregnant sister, her husband, and my oldest niece, Jaimie, I was presented with a plane ticket to Arizona, purchased by my sister.

Arizona is where my maternal aunts and their husbands and children lived. No one asked me did I want to go; I was literally packed up and flown out without so much as a conversation...I honestly don't even think they cared. For the umpteenth time in my life, I was being treated like an inconvenience that needed to be handled, yet again. This was not the first time I had been whisked away on a flight to Arizona, after a death in the family.

Back in 1988, I was sent to Arizona after my maternal grandmother died. It was my very first flight, and I was sent alone. At eight years old, I was nervous and had to deal with feelings of being abandoned and rejected at a time when I needed to be surrounded by assurance and comfort, all on my own. I believe my grieving process was not validated or even thought of simply because of my age. However, my feelings were real and raw, and I too had lost someone when my grandmother died. Truthfully, she was an integral part of my childhood; at one point, due to a house fire that caused us to be displaced, me, my sister, and mother lived with my grandmother. She often watched me while my mother worked, and we all attended church together. Unfortunately, my grandmother succumbed to uterine cancer, but during the course of her battle with it, she lived with us. She received hospice care right there in our living room, hospital bed and all. Though she was sick, I talked to her daily, and even on her sickbed, we would play games with one another. How my feelings and thoughts surrounding her death got lost in the shuffle with my mother is hard for me to determine; lack of knowledge, perhaps? Or, maybe, the adults in my world were too absorbed with their own grieving to consider mine.

I often reflect back to whether or not I was a needy or pesky child, and I do not believe so, talkative at most. From the stories I recall hearing about me growing up, I do not believe that was the case. In fact, I have been told that I often was very quiet, very shy, and spent lots of time alone and out of the way. However, even if that were not the case, if I just so happened to be needy or clingy or draining--I was a child that needed comfort, reassurance, validation, and to feel wanted. In this particular case as with others, I didn't receive that.

My adult-mind tells me that the trip was not necessarily because I was an irritant but because my mother just needed one less thing to worry about. Regardless, whichever way you slice it, it still was poorly executed. Sending me away definitely affected me at that time and only reinforced the feelings of rejection and abandonment that were already looming and festering inside of me that stemmed from previous instances including the separation of my parents, the disappearing act of my father, and the verbal recording of my inner voice reminding me of my sister's declaration: that "Mama cried nearly every day of her pregnancy with you," because she did not want to be pregnant. Those feelings were being relived all over again, even at the tender age of eight.

At fifteen years' old, nothing had changed, and needless to say, I was devastated by the new turn of events and had several questions. Questions like, why am I being sent here? And, for how long? Those answers were never given to me. I believe my sister's plan was to leave me there, that is until my father spoke up.

My father resurfaced only after my mother died and decided that he should be back in Chicago with me. He had spent the majority of my childhood living a life on the east coast that I had, and still have, no clue about. As my memory serves it, I can count on one hand the number of times I saw him once my parents split. Once was at the age of four, I still remember it like yesterday. He propped me up on a pillow in his lap behind the wheel of his car, and he let me steer, while he pushed the gas pedal. We rode down the middle of our block, and I felt on top of the world. There in that car he made promises to me; promises that would on the surface soon be forgotten but still remain planted in my subconscious. My daddy told me that him and my mother were separating, but he would still come to see me. He told me that he would visit and that he wouldn't leave me. As a little girl, innocent of the world and all the problems that came along with being a daddy-less daughter, I believed him. I had no reason not to—until he showed me. Granted, there were times when we would talk on the phone, but those memories soon faded, and the connection between us was lost. He didn't come back for his little girl.

The next time I would see my father would be at my 12th birthday party. That year, my mother allowed me to have a sleepover. When I awoke, my father was in the kitchen sitting casually with my mother talking. I was excited to see him and had soon forgotten about all the time that had elapsed between us. That is the funny thing about kids and parents…seems as though all a parent has to do is show up, and everything is okay; all is forgiven, and the love still exists. That trip he made to Chicago wasn't long, he probably stayed an additional two days or so. He bought me some winter boots, and just as quickly as he came in, he was back out of my life again.

So, while my dad and I did not have a "relationship," per se, I was happy to have him back at the age of fifteen. We hadn't communicated in years so naturally things were kind of weird at first. My father was not the best in easing into situations. He had a very demanding nature and wanted immediate respect and an instant relationship between us. Talk about expectations! I was again overwhelmed with life and what it was bringing directly to my front door, even if it was a mending of an old relationship with my father. As a teen learning to navigate life and coping with my mother's death, how could anyone blame me?

Rejection and abandonment both have a way of growing so steadily that if you are not careful, you will look up and find that you have a full-grown root of bitterness and mistrust. These awful spirits manifest in so many different ways that a person can have a hard time tracing it back to where it all started and choose to give it up, because it feels so hopeless. For me, those feelings of rejection and abandonment manifested in the forms of bitterness, distrust, and anger. I often times had an unpleasant attitude while at home, in addition to the average growing pains of a regularly developing teenager. Life was not the best for me.

I spent roughly six weeks in Arizona and returned back to my new "home" with everything running smoothly and in full swing. My nephew was born a couple weeks after my return. Babies have their own special way of altering a home. Little did I know, it would also alter my lifestyle as well. I was happy that my nephew had entered the world and wanted nothing more than to be a part of his, that is until the separation came.

Because I was excited about the birth of RJ and everything surrounding him, I wanted to give him a nickname. The nickname I came up with was not liked at all by my brother-in-law, and he snapped in such a way that I purposely chose to distance myself from my nephew and from their family. I felt as though I was not a true part of their family nucleus, and in reality, I was not. Ryan informed me that RJ was his son, and he did not like the nickname that I had chosen and I was to not, under any circumstances, call him by that name. In hindsight, as a mother of 4, I get it; however, as a 15-year-old girl, trying to fit into a family that seemingly did not want me there, it was hurtful. The decisions that I made at that time surrounding my level of closeness with my nephew and even my second-born niece, Janiya, are still evident to this day. Residual hurt from that incident and a plethora of others, eventually affected the closeness that I would have liked to have had with both my nieces and nephew.

My firstborn niece spent the first two years of her life under the same roof as me and my mother along with my sister. She and I have an unbreakable bond that will last until the end of time. There was no interference when we bonded, and she actually was like a little sister/first baby to me. Ironically, she and I are also twelve years apart, like my sister and I. Because that relationship grew unhindered, there is a deeper understanding of her on more levels than with the other two, that I continue to nourish and grow even now.

Due to the interference of how I chose to bond with my nephew, he merely became a chore in the house. Yet another thing I was mandated to assist my sister with in her home. The emotions and attachment had been removed, and I was going through the motions. Please don't mistake for one moment that I do not love the other two, because I do (with all I have inside), but unfortunately,

I allowed rejection and abandonment to stifle the bond that could have been something much greater, much like with my first niece. As of late, I believe that the connection with my second niece is developing. The dynamics between she and I are changing and for that I am grateful.

After a while, I gathered the notion that I was nothing more than "the help." My new place of residence was a 3-bedroom, 2-bathroom tri-level, probably no more than 1200 square feet, and I was made responsible for cleaning about 600 square feet of it. My chores included, but were not limited to: washing breakfast, lunch, and dinner dishes; vacuuming three times weekly (this included sweeping the carpeted stairs and vacuuming the hall and landing); dusting three times weekly; cleaning the guest bathroom two times weekly; washing my clothes; watering the plants; cleaning my room; boiling baby bottles; making baby formula; most days starting dinner, sweeping, mopping; and lastly, being an on-call babysitter, without as much as a request. I was told that I was not responsible for the main bathroom because she wanted it cleaned a "certain way." Even with all of that, I was nit-picked over trivial things like food, not being allowed more than one piece of meat (turkey-bologna) on a sandwich or having snacks through the course of the day. I was clear that I was not welcomed and certainly was not appreciated.

The latter part of the summer of '96, I was shuffled into a volunteer job with our church's summer camp and that took up the majority of my day. However, I was frustrated at the idea of getting up and "going to work" at my age without so much as a couple dollars to show for it. It was just another example of sticking me somewhere that I did not want to be because I was an inconvenience to someone else.

While being in the new neighborhood for a little while, I remembered that an old "puppy-love" boyfriend had moved to the surrounding area, and after a little research, I found him. I met Omari when I was twelve years old, while working on a school project with my classmate. Omari had recently relocated and now lived near the church I was volunteering at. While it was in walking distance, it was still somewhat of a hike.

Omari and I were girlfriend and boyfriend for roughly two or three months and only saw each other one other time aside from our initial meeting. We met at the local library to visit with each other and shared our first kiss, typical for our age group. Over the course of our short-lived puppy-love "relationship," I discovered he had a host of other girlfriends and admirers, one of them being my good friend, who was actually the one who introduced us. Needless to say, the relationship with Omari ended, and my friend and I were never the same after that.

I choose to take this walk down memory lane not to rehash old stuff—but to give credence to the cycle of abandonment and rejection in a person's life and how it can pop up at any given opportunity, if they choose to wear it as a garment. Because I was young, I cannot fault myself for wearing the ugliness of rejection, abandonment, and unforgiveness, but as we grow in physical stature, we must also grow in intellect and emotional stature. To allow past situations in our lives to manipulate us into being or living a life that we are not called to live is not living at all. Letting go of the former things and choosing to see how adversity can push one toward greatness is what should be the focus.

For me, reconnecting with the former puppy-love boyfriend was a reach back to something familiar, something that reminded me of home and what I used to know. Unfortunately, it was also an indication that I lacked proper self-love and self-esteem. I was choosing to return or reconnect with someone who had not only rejected and embarrassed me but also contributed to severing a friendship. Not realizing the flaw in this decision-making process eventually cost me.

Some past experiences need not be resurrected, recreated, recycled, or relived! Live in purpose, not pain.

—*Carsen Aminna*

3

VULNERABLE

So much had changed with Omari, and I soon discovered, the experienced sixteen-year-old teen I met up with on the block of his father's house, was not the same thirteen-year-old boy I had met, just a few years back. I was only looking for a friend, but unbeknownst to me, he had so much more on his mind and in his plans, and all of it was lustful. Going through the grieving process and carrying baggage from my early childhood, in addition to the rejection I was receiving at home, left me vulnerable to many things, false hope, unhealthy attachments, and above all, manipulation.

Omari was open about having a girlfriend, and I was completely okay with that because I initially did not want him in that way. He would go on and on about how crazy and volatile his girlfriend was and claimed that it was all in her head, and as his friend, I listened. He often times painted her as being unstable and emotionally unwrapped, and again, I listened. He blamed most of their relationship troubles on the death of her father and said that something in her changed from the first time they met in the eighth grade.

Because we now attended the same high school, we remained connected over the course of the next two years. Most of our conversations were done in secret, and I dared not speak to him in the hall. His girlfriend had friends, rather secret agents, and they would report any and all of his activities, if spotted during the course of a school day. While the friendship between Omari and I was completely platonic on my end, his girlfriend definitely saw things another way. A few times, there was talk of her not liking me, thinking that him and I were cheating, but luckily, things never progressed further than that. How silly would it have been to get into an altercation over a boy that I wasn't involved with!

Besides Omari having a girlfriend, I had a boyfriend as well. I never wanted to disrespect anything that my boyfriend and I shared, but being so sheltered and not being allowed out of the house much, left me desiring more. I wanted to go on dates and attend dances without having to sneak, but most of that was an unfulfilled want. Just as much pressure as it was on me to want to see my boyfriend, it was pressure on him. He often expressed how boring it was not being able to see me, or come by the house, and I agreed. I remember feeling so stifled and above all, untrusted and for no reason.

During mine and Omari's time in school, I was his sounding board and a constant in his life. I provided a space for him to talk and share, but nothing more.

Little did I know, most of his girlfriend's behavior was the direct result of his promiscuity and lying. They eventually became pregnant their senior year, and boy, was I in for a ride. I took a lot of what he said to me concerning her at face value and never questioned the legitimacy of his words, because honestly, her actions matched up with all of them, but I always questioned in the back of my mind, what was he doing to get the reactions she was giving? All too soon I would find out.

In our friendship, there was always an underlining press about us being more than friends, but thankfully, I had enough pride to not want to play "second fiddle." That concept was impressed upon me very early in life, by my mother, along with the understanding that I had only one name and I had better keep it clean. That meant don't whore around and remember that I am a lady at all times; I should always be treated with respect, and if I have to be any man's (in this case, boy) secret, then surely, I wasn't the young lady for him.

Two are better than one, because they
have a good return for their labor: If
either of them falls down, one can help
the other up. But pity anyone who falls
and has no one to help them up.

-Ecclesiastes 4: 9-10 (KJV)

4

FROM A HAWK TO A FALCON

My summer came to an uneventful end, and as the new school year arrived in full-swing, I came to the absolute conclusion that I did not fit in at my new school and I was completely disinterested in trying to do so. Believe it or not, despite my hometown just being twenty minutes south of where I now lived, it was an extreme culture shock for me, and I had problems adjusting to the loud, rude, and aggressive behaviors that came with the new crowd of kids. The girls were different, way more abrasive, and the guys were different, too; they were way more mannish.

I dressed, talked, and acted differently from all of them. By all intents and purposes, I was considered what we referred to as "lame." I was not a part of the "cool kids" and didn't pretend to be. I had no desire to drink, smoke weed, ditch school, or take part in sex with random guys and then talk about it in homeroom, like my new peers. By no means, did I assume that my way was better; it was just not the same.

Being the new kid was a painful task that I just was not up for. There was too much to think about, too much to consider, and other than a childhood puppy-love ex with a "crazed, maniac girlfriend," I knew absolutely, positively no one in the school. Coming to class everyday was overwhelming, after fighting through the halls with nearly 200-300 more kids than I was used to; I had to endure ridicule from immature boys that openly teased me about my chipped tooth and skinny frame, not to mention the decision to rock a more "mature" hairstyle that was a "pixie cut." While it was a cute haircut and worn by favorited artist and actresses, it was not readily accepted by immature boys in high-school.

One boy, in particular in my Geometry class, would hassle me every single day. He would tease and poke fun about everything from my hair to my clothes. The whole class would laugh, and because I was not used to having to defend myself in that way, I sat there and I took it. The most I would say was "shut up" and roll my eyes. I was actively being bullied and never told a soul. Having to endure bullying and being singled out was absolutely taxing on my emotional state, and most days, I was not comfortable in my own skin—at least not in those particular classes where my physical appearance was being scrutinized for an entire fifty minutes or so.

Usually, by a teen's sophomore year, they have found their tribe and placed boundaries between themselves and their enemies, but for me in this new environment, I was just getting started. I was behind the 8-ball because I hadn't grown up in the neighborhood or attended any of the middle schools that the other students came from. Being the "new girl" affords you two things: one, unasked-for attention from the guys, and two, because you are perceived as a threat because you're new, uncalled-for remarks of jealousy and nasty attitudes from the girls. I did not want or ask for either.

It was arranged for me to try out for the pom-pons squad by Leah and some other connects within the school district. In hindsight, it was a very wise and strategic move on their behalf, but I could have melted in embarrassment and sheer anguish that the situation provided. With my participation in an after-school activity, I had to maintain my G.P.A. and it also helped me to find my own tribe, of sorts. Involvement was key, whether I deemed it good for me or not.

I found a really good friend in two girls, Angela and Katrina, who were sophomores as well.

Angela was a flag girl, and Katrina was on the pom-pon squad with me. We shared everything with one another, and they proved themselves trustworthy. I cherished those friendships, even today because they truly helped me find my way. They would often confirm for me that the girls who ridiculed or teased me were just unpleasant as a whole or jealous and reassured me that it wasn't just me, and also gave me advice on situations with guys. Unfortunately, there were more girls that created problems for me or disliked me than ones that had my back, but such is life. In fact, those first couple of years on the pom-pon squad were hurtful and frustrating. Having to deal with captains that were mean, rude and quick to embarrass you for the sake of being cool is a hard task. It makes you grow a thick skin. I was careful not to be like them and chose to treat every girl on the squad with respect, regardless of their dance skills, personality, or body type.

It's so important for a young girl to guard her heart and surround herself with other girls that affirm her and show themselves friendly; it can make all the difference in how she perceives herself and how she perceives the world around her. Because hindsight is always 20/20, I now know that most of those girls that were mean to me were struggling with insecurities and lack of self-love themselves. Everything they said and did to me were merely reflections of what they felt about themselves. Every cutting word, every snide remark, every rumor passed, every public and private slight, were things that they were dealing with on the inside. Most of them didn't know my story or my pain: they never asked, and I never shared. I have never been one to really divulge all my personal business, and I certainly did not require an audience of pity. I wanted people to treat me exactly like they felt they should, disregarding my circumstances- otherwise, I felt it would have been forced and insincere. Sadly, the majority chose to be mean.

Once I became captain of my pom-pon team (as an upperclassman), the atmosphere shifted within our squad. With me and Katrina being in leadership, there was a sense of compassion on the team, and there were no big "I's" and little "you's." For the most part, all of the girls liked us, and those that didn't, in later years, came to apologize for the difficult time they gave me and said once they filled my shoes they understood why I was so hard on them.

My experience in leadership, even in high school, afforded me the ability to begin to understand people and how their home situations affected who they were outside of the home. I became aware that my circumstance wasn't unique to just me and that others experienced similar events. During the course of a three-year span, we had on our team: girls who were wards of the state, sexually abused, the socially awkward, teen mothers, and those who choose to terminate their pregnancies, as well as those who came from homes where the parents didn't care what they did. We were a group of perfectly, imperfect young ladies that came together to form a team, and we came together well. I learned a lot about myself during those years, and those lessons still remain to this day, as well as some of those friendships.

Throughout all the transitions that took place in my life, one thing that did not suffer was my grades. I felt my grades were a direct reflection of me. While I didn't feel immense pressure about them, I always was consistent about handing in homework and doing well on tests. I was an average student, a few A's here and there, but mostly B's and some C's, and no matter the circumstances, that never faltered. However, the stress in my house was so intense that I wanted out, and I stopped being concerned about grades and began to focus more on getting out.

Near the beginning of my junior year, I became immensely frustrated with my living situation and made the bold and very unwise decision to run away from home. It was a poorly thought-out plan, and I was found the very next day. I had decided to hide out at my then boyfriend, Romel's house. Romel's father was aware that I was there and welcomed my presence. He was aware of all the drama that was taking place in my household and honestly, just wanted to rescue me; however, that definitely was not the place for me to be. After just one night of me being missing, a very close friend of the family, whom we had adopted as an "aunt," showed up to my boyfriend's house the next morning bright and early with a voice as loud as thunder and a fist that pounded down like rain against the front door. She called out and banged for nearly two hours to no avail. I was not going to budge unless I was forced. Finally, a phone call was made to Romel's father by either Leah or my "aunt," and he was told that if I didn't leave his home, he would have the police at his front door, ready to arrest him for harboring a minor. Needless to say, because we didn't want his father getting into any trouble, I begrudgingly came out. I absolutely, positively, just wanted to be left alone. I was promptly put on punishment and forbidden to see Romel again.

The truth was, it wasn't my boyfriend's idea, it was mine. Had I had another household to retreat to that was as free-flowing as his, I would have gone there as well. I merely was seeking refuge, an asylum from the hell I was living through, in my sister's house. Instead of being talked to, I was talked at. Instead of being truly heard, I was merely listened to. Instead of Leah and Ryan taking ownership of their hand in the situation, I was handed the blame in its entirety. Could my feelings of frustration and hurt have been handled differently? Sure, they could have…with the proper supports. Where there is no platform for a person to express themselves, especially a teen-- there you will discover poorly executed decisions and unsavory behaviors.

When you're a young girl and you're in whatever version of what you think love is, anyone that tries to break that up is the enemy. The truth of the matter is my sister was right. Romel was, in general, a good guy, but he wasn't good for me. He had his own rejection and abandonment issues to address; and I surely had no need for his on top of mine. However, in life, that which we are is that which we attract. Because I was broken and needed to heal in many places, I attracted broken people. What we don't address will continue to be our mess.

When we are at our weakest, we are
actually being made strong; we learn
from these moments and grow.
Where space and time is needed—
It must be given.
Less the lesson be in vain.

-Carsen Aminna

5

HOME, NOT SO SWEET HOME

As time progressed, the situation in my house was getting worse. I had my behavioral ups and downs during the course of the school year but nothing major. I worked a lot once I turned seventeen and was rarely home. In fact, at one point, I had three jobs and no car. Between public transportation and an occasional ride here and there from my sister or my brother-in-law, I made it happen.

Let me be the first to say that I was every bit of a teenager, I shirked chores from time to time, I gave attitude sometimes unnecessarily, and I loved talking on the phone. All these are rites of passage for teens, and I was no different. In fact, I would like to say that I was immensely well-behaved, considering the circumstances; after all, Leah was my sister and not my mother. Truthfully, I viewed us as really equal in a lot of ways, but because the lines were blurred due to my mother's death, the equality was construed.

The unfortunate part is that I suffered a great deal in that house. There were no warm and fuzzy sister moments or random "girl's night." I was met with stringent chore charts, a series of "aunty duties" to perform for two small children and very little freedom. A great majority of places I requested to go or things I asked if I could do were met with hard, cold, "no's." What I didn't know at the time was that Leah was "parenting" me from a place of fear and also resentment. Ryan only added fuel to the fire with condescending conversations and inappropriately timed sarcasm. My pushback to the heavily-guarded and overly-structured treatment was written off as rebellion and issues centered around my mother's death, and I was promptly ushered into counseling.

Honestly, counseling at that point in my life was a sincere, one-hundred percent waste of time and money. I could have thought of a million other places that I would much rather have been than to be sitting across from some woman that I didn't know, hurling a diagnosis of depression at me. I was angry at the label, I was angry that no one was listening, I was angry that no one seemed to care, and I was angry that my life had been turned upside down and I had no control over any of it. After about three sessions maybe four, my counselor asked me why didn't I talk and if I wanted to be there. I told her that I had nothing to say, and honestly, I didn't want to be there. Needless to say, the sessions discontinued, and nothing changed in the house.

Counseling is a tricky thing; as much good as it can do, it can also do nothing at all if the client is not a willing participant in the process. Parents, guardians, caregivers, and teens, as well, need to know that healing and grieving takes time; it is a process that looks and feels different on everyone. Sometimes, counseling is mandatory; other times, it's a nice side dish to an otherwise healthy, developmental process. Using mindfulness to gauge that meter of need is imperative. What would have worked for me as an emotionally battered teen would have been a simple clarification of my sister's true thoughts and feelings regarding our mother's death and the residual feelings surrounding it. I believe it would have most likely afforded us the luxury of actually liking each other, during the short time I was in her home. Instead, her denial of her true feelings allowed for distrust, misuse of sisterhood, and flawed thinking on each of our behalves.

With my first "runaway" under my belt and my sister's looming distaste for Romel, I felt I had no one to talk to. My childhood friends that I had known since I was about seven years old were not coming through for me like I thought they should, and the brokenness between Leah and I left me sincerely depleted. It seemed at that point in my life there was a never-ending road to my unhappiness; one where my sister and brother-in-law were blazing the path.

With a combination of a fizzled-out first- love, major disconnect from my old neighborhood and friends, and no letup in the house, I was becoming a ticking time-bomb. The one constant in my life was my church youth group. I attended a youth group with my childhood friends from my old neighborhood every Wednesday, and that truthfully was about the only time I saw them. They rarely came to see me, and I believe that had more to do with Leah's unwelcoming attitude of company in her home. I don't think my friends necessarily felt comfortable being there. I simply cannot fault them for not wanting to frequent the house. No one wants to visit with someone where they are obviously being just tolerated.

During the three years that I attended youth group, I dated three guys, one of which ended up murdering someone years later. He never was mean to me; in fact, I was the only one that could calm him down in his fits of anger. Our relationship didn't last very long; however, again, it speaks to the brokenness that I was attracting. The other two young men rejected me because I was not sexually active, and despite us all being "Christians" and attending church once a week and for me twice, they still applied the pressure of sex. One chose to embarrass me by bringing his new girlfriend to church without breaking up with me first; and the other chose to embarrass me by having sex with and taking degrading pictures of a girl that was supposed to be my friend. Ultimately, I am glad I made the decisions that I made as a teen especially concerning the latter two guys; however, at that time, it did not take away the sting of being rejected and embarrassed, once more. I repeatedly found myself involved with guys that sought out to purposefully reject and embarrass me publicly. It was an unidentified pattern that I was involved in and completely unaware of.

The flip-side to this youth group coin is that we had a husband and wife team that led us in our Bible study. Naturally, the wife spoke to the girls about certain things, and the husband spoke to the guys about stuff. The wife and I never really saw eye to eye. While she worked with youth in our church, it is my belief that she had never fully forgiven herself for her indiscretions as a youth and consistently projected them on the girls in our group, more specifically me. I hated to be misjudged, and she had immensely misjudged me. This woman had her thoughts about me based on assumptions and her own personal life experiences, and it was reflected in the way she spoke to me and in the way she treated me.

One of the most defining times in my teenage youth was being excluded from an event that was for young girls in our youth group to learn more about Christ on a deeper level and walking in leadership. I was later told that she assumed I was sexually active and that I would have had no place in a function of that sort. The average teen probably wouldn't have cared about a Christian leadership camp, but for me, it meant everything. I was in a time in my life where finding God and my purpose in Him was important to me. Having that door shut in my face facilitated the building of a wall in my heart that made it easy for me to harbor unforgiveness for her and others, who like her misjudged and rejected me.

Yet again, rejection loomed, chased, and hung over me like a dark cloud. I was hard-pressed to find a place of peace or solace, and many nights, I cried myself to sleep, just asking why. With a newfound hurt under my belt, I dug in even further with not liking my youth group leader and completely avoided her at all cost. In later years, I discovered some tidbits of her past, and I understood that she was projecting onto me issues that she had within herself. However, to a teenage girl like myself who was struggling in every facet of my life and just looking for someone to accept me for who I truly was, it was just another example of why shutting down felt better, why going numb worked better in my favor, and why getting close to people in an attempt to forge a friendship only proved unpromising.

My youth group leader missed an opportunity to pour into me whatever it is she felt she missed in her teenage years and also an opportunity to encourage, edify, and assist in healing a budding young woman. Much of what she attempted to instruct us girls on was lost on me because her cutting actions and words towards me spoke way louder than her teachings.

During this time, I had my first full-blown experience with grief. There on the living-room floor of my sister and brother-in-law's home, I let it all out. I was home alone for a little while, and suddenly without warning, it hit me. If, by chance, you are reading this and have never experienced the death of someone you truly love and are close to, what I am about to express is intangible. It is intangible because there is no other pain like it. Unless you have experienced it, you cannot empathize; it is impossible. It is an emotional pain that is so profound that it hurts physically. Try to imagine having your feelings hurt so bad that you feel it in your body. Intangible, right? That feeling, that pain that resonated through my entire being allowed space for me to unashamedly roll around on the floor, until I was all cried out. It also allowed God to begin to heal me in the places that I had not been given the space and opportunity to do so prior.

By my junior year, I worked so much so that I was never at home, and it was all very strategic and very purposeful. Not being home provided me with a sense of release from the heaviness that overcame me when I was there. However, those times when I was at home, I felt as though both Leah and Ryan found fault in me. The feeling of never being satisfactory, not trusted, and a burden sat right in the middle of my chest and lived. It stayed longer than I would have liked and created a person within myself that was not who I now know God created me to be. The year rolled in like a tide and crashed. I had no real plans for the future in regards to education and/or a career after high school. I believe my lack of plans spoke to what I was feeling in my heart. I just wanted things to stay the same. Even if I was broken, it was familiar. This concept is not foreign to people who live in dysfunction and pain, especially when feelings of abandonment rule over their judgment. The need to just remain in sameness because everything else is so uncertain is where I lived.

Restoration heals the heartsick;
it is a balm to the soul.

-Carsen Aminna

6

SENIOR FLIGHT

I cannot tell a lie, my schedule for my senior year was pretty dope. I started school about 7:45 am and was done with my day and walking out the door at 11:10 am. I was driving by this time and would often stop to grab something to eat and visit with Omari. We started dating my senior year of high school. He had finally dissolved his tumultuous relationship with his child's mother, and we were on the road to forever, or so I thought.

Little did I know that within a matter of a year, the young man that courted me so vigorously would be my husband, and we would have a child together. That time in my life was pretty golden, and I felt a sense of "light-at-the-end-of-the-tunnel." Feelings and emotions in my home were still pretty intense amongst us all, and my level of comfortability was still flat-lined at zero.

With so much going on in my present life, I had not had the chance to focus properly on my future. As fall turned into winter, the weight of my home situation became all too much for me to bear, and I began to think about leaving again. While in the work-program in school, I became friends with a few girls, one who would change the course of the remainder of my high school year, Andrea. In one of our many conversations about my much-hated living situation, she offered to speak to her mother on my behalf to see if I could live with them from March until I graduated. I couldn't have been more delighted. Andrea was a good girl and a good friend; she was very smart and had several prospective schools in which to choose from. Her future was in her hands. I yearned for the confidence and assuredness she had in her future, but sadly, life had either taken some of that from me or never provided it in the first place.

As promised, she talked to her mom on my behalf, and her mother agreed to help. There were no legal issues to hash out and no police to call this time, because I was eighteen. From the time I found out the news, which was in the latter part of February, up until the week before the Saturday in which I planned to move, I began to pack my things. I also began holding onto more money than I normally would have and made plans more solidly about my secondary education. I had sent off a few applications and gotten a few offers but hadn't made a concrete decision.

While there were several incidents that led up to me leaving my sister's house, one or two stand out to me in particular. For instance, the time she demanded that I try on my prom dress. Because

I was not up for her ridicule and tearing down of my self-esteem, I refused. Granted, the dress was a little risqué and pushed the envelope on what was allowed for a school prom; it still was no cause to attack me in the fashion in which she did. My refusal frustrated her to the point of trying to put on my prom dress, herself. The visual remains very clear to me to this very day. She was enraged at the idea of me not doing something she told me to do. In her fit of incomprehensible rage, she yanked off her pajama gown threw it to her bed and proceeded to pull, tug, yank, and force her body into a custom-designed and fitted evening gown that was not hers. She attempted to put on the dress sitting, standing, and lastly, bent over-- head over her knees at the foot of her bed, while I looked on in horror. She finally realized, she was not getting in the dress. Leah and I have always been close to each other in size, but never the same, she has always been bigger and taller than me, and I was consequently melting from the fear of her damaging my gown and having to spend additional money to have it fixed. Her inability to control me was I think the most enraging thing to her; and the idea of someone who claimed to love me, wanting to control me, was mine.

I will never forget the few days leading up to me leaving my sister's home. She had accidentally discovered I had packed up my entire room and began to question me. I told her matter-of-factly I was moving out, that Saturday. She repeated what I said in disbelief and immediately began asking questions about where I would stay and what I could and couldn't have. None of it phased me. I was emotionally drained from the torment I was experiencing in her home, and at that point, nothing she could say or do could affect me any longer. I was told the car that I put a brand new battery in, and my father worked so diligently on with his time and money was one of the things that I could not have. Granted, the car was given to me by Ryan; however, he received it for little to nothing from his step-father, and between myself and my father, we had done all the work to get it running. That still did not stop me. In fact, it only made me hustle that much harder.

By late May, early June, I had a newer, well-running, cleaner version of the same car that they took from me. What I learned in time was that God's grace is surely sufficient, and when the enemy comes to steal, kill, and destroy, God always replaces the thing with something better, and it comes at no great cost to you. He is a redeemer of all things. The situation also gave me a different perspective on my sister and the mental and emotional place that she was in. I can't say that I was willing to forgive and forget at all; I was just aware.

Time unfolded beautifully in the Smith household. Upon staying in my friend's home, I did my very best to be a part and contribute to the household. I was truly used to doing most, if not all of the cleaning and some of the cooking or at minimum preparation for dinner in my sister's home. I was told lovingly that was not the expectation of me while living in my new arrangement. I was told that in exchange for a roof over my head and food in my stomach, good grades and staying out of trouble was my penance. This was an absolutely foreign concept to me, but I was definitely okay with it! Not having to wash, dry, and put up dishes; boil baby bottles; mix infant formula; prepare dinner; vacuum; sweep; mop; clean bathrooms; and wash clothes; or babysit was a breath of fresh air. I was only responsible for me and my mess! I almost didn't know what to do with myself!

In addition to being released from household chores, I was given a reasonable curfew and permission to come and go as long as I informed Mrs. Smith of my whereabouts and with whom I would be with. I finally felt validated, trusted, and heard. I was in an environment where I was welcomed, and it made all the difference within me, even in that little amount of time.

As planned, I attended prom with Omari and friends, and graduated with somewhat of a vision. Three out of the four colleges I applied to accepted me, and I decided on attending at a local university. It was definitely not my family's favorite pick, but it was my choice, nonetheless. Andrea and I had a conjoined graduation party that was really nice. Some of my family and friends came to celebrate and wish me well, while others choose not to. I ended the night with Omari at a local restaurant, just down the street from our high school. We discussed our plans for the future and enjoyed each other's company, until it was time to go home.

After graduation, I worked the entire summer and continually prepared for the journey that lay ahead of me. I did not have a great deal of support in terms of school because of where I chose to attend. I saved up as much as I could and purchased the majority of my dorm necessities by myself. Condescending thoughts often filled phone conversations between Leah and I. Our meet and greets pertaining to my school choice were always laced with "it's not too late" speeches. Never once did family offer to just meet me where I was, but consistently tried to change the plans that I had laid out for myself. When it came to filing for financial aid, I was on my own. I had never filled out a financial aid form before and took it upon myself to figure it out, and I did. I asked my sister to ask our grandfather could he help with the cost of my books; it was the only thing my financial aid was unable to cover. He returned with an outright, "no," for an answer. Leah shared with me that our grandfather, whom I had never asked for anything before, said he was uncertain on where I would be spending the money. I had never asked him for anything before and never did again. With more bitterness in my heart, I was forced to take out a loan, something I absolutely did not want to do. My eyes were opened yet again to the fact that I had no one who truly had my back when it was up against a wall. There is no doubt in my mind that whether my mother had the means for my books or not, she would have found a way for me to get them—without the loan. Situations like this often surfaced in my life, and time and time again, the ones that were my family and friends never seemed to come through; despite my availability and support to them financially, emotionally, and any other way possible. However, I am crystal clear that it has only made me stronger, more responsible, and yet again even more resilient.

I fed on your twisted words of manipulation
Broken--each of the promises made
Small and sharp pieces, they were
Immaculately wrapped in a bow with
a ring attached, baby in tow.

-Carsen Aminna

7

CHANGES

Freshman year in college was interesting, to say the least. I truly was sheltered from most things in life, and even though by this time I was admittingly sexually active with Omari, there were things that I just didn't do and certainly didn't talk about with others. I met some cool people at CSU and some I would much rather forget.

I began my college career with the idea that I should major in Education: Elementary Education to be exact. Notice I said "should." The thread of constantly trying to appease those around me, that seemed to be consistently displeased with my decision, continually appeared throughout my journey to womanhood. Deep in my heart, I had no real true desire to be a schoolteacher. However, I was told by my "aunt" and my sister that I would always have a job if I went the route of being an Educator. So, while walking along my own path, I compromised. I didn't look into the desires of my own heart, and unfortunately, I was not seeking God for direction either. I was so tired of fighting at every turn that I decided to just go with the flow, concerning my major and hope for some alliances with my family to come of it.

As incoming freshman, we were all on the first floor of the residency hall, and truthfully that is where I stayed. I was so very closed off to people and new things that I literally only went to one other floor in a four-floor building, one time during the entire first semester. While everyone else was getting high and drunk and having sex with multiple people, I was holed up in my room. If I wasn't in my room, I was somewhere with

Omari, spending time. We became closer and closer, and I was completely unaware that I was being spun into a web of manipulation.

The unfortunate part about being manipulated is often times the person being manipulated very seldom sees it before it is too late. This was the case with me. One of the things that I kept with me from my mother's house was a desktop computer. I was thankful and grateful to have it, because laptops were overly expensive at the time, and the computer lab in our residency hall at school could be overwhelming for me at times.

On my desktop, I kept a digital journal. I typed in it almost every day. In it were the secrets of my heart and my inner-deepest feelings. Omari caught wind of that and took it upon himself to explore my journal, whenever he could sneak a look. One of the desires of my heart poured out on my computer screen was to have a family. I wanted to be married and have children, but of course, all within a sensible amount of time. For me, there was no real rush, just the hope of the possibility.

Honestly, at that point in my life, I had not put any one suitor in that "husband" role; it was merely a desire. Even though I was dating Omari, I didn't entertain him as a possible husband.

Upon reading what I wanted in my life, Omari questioned the validity of my writings and proposed that we could be married and have children, if I desired to do so with him. Being faced with the idea of someone actually wanting forever with me, allegedly with no strings attached, and desiring to build a life with me because they loved me was music to my ears. I finally felt loved. After fighting through years of rejection, perceived and actual abandonment, emotional torment and pain, I believed he was my savior; the one to come along and redeem me. Little did I know, we were both looking for something that neither one of us could provide for one another, and his incompleteness would manifest into abuse.

Our first steps in deciding our future were to talk it through and plan, plan for jobs, plan for housing, and plan for a baby. In our planning, we also desired the blessing of our families. Despite what my family had and had not been to me in the past, I still wanted approval. Approval that was never given. Omari and I set out to speak with my sister about our plans to be married, and she listened, and she disapproved; and rightfully so. We were absolutely, positively too young. We hardly knew ourselves, and even after one year of serious dating, we honestly didn't know each other. However, both of us were too stubborn and too rebellious to hear the sound wisdom that she was speaking.

After about six weeks of actively trying to get pregnant, basically in order to spite everyone that told us no, we conceived. While we were immensely overjoyed with our actions, we were also unprepared. It is amazing how we can purposefully put the cart before the horse and be shocked when things don't pan out the way we thought they would. Once I shared with Leah my pregnancy, she revealed her disappointment and concern about my future. She asked me about the plans we were making and was marriage still the goal. I expressed to her that it was never really off the table, but we were discouraged because we hadn't received her blessing. She left me with the understanding that ultimately it was my decision, but that I had choices and each choice had a consequence. I was relieved that I had gotten the news off my chest and began to be more comfortable with moving forward with my new life, with my soon-to-be husband, and baby.

As the nearing of the end of my first semester in college approached, I was in full-on failure mode. The pregnancy symptoms that I was experiencing were the only thing I could focus on. I stopped attending class, couldn't eat most days, and remained in a state of nausea. I had never experienced the idea of not caring about my education. It was a foreign concept, and while it was real because I was experiencing it, I couldn't fully understand why. I was not pleased with the outcome of my choosing to fail but was not discouraged about dusting myself off and trying again. I shared with no one that after an entire semester out of fifteen credit hours I was walking away with only three credit hours, and sadly that grade was a D. I was ashamed and disappointed in myself and didn't need the continuum of a verbal beat-down I knew I would receive if I revealed to my family I had failed.

Sharing the news with my childhood friends about my pregnancy was actually more devastating than telling my sister. I can't say what I expected to hear from them, but I can say that I didn't believe that I would be met with the amount of disapproval that I was. Truthfully, many things had already changed in our friendship, and by my senior year of high school, I had been replaced by another girl. None of us really talked about it, it was just done. So, while I was happy about my new life unfolding and all the new possibilities, I was also saddened by the fact that my childhood friends and I were pretty much done being friends. I never wanted that aspect of my life to change, and while it was flimsy at best, it was still a constant.

Omari and I were married in January of 2000, and I experienced my first bout with emotional distress within the following 2 weeks of our marriage. As the result of a very minor disagreement, he destroyed our belongings and the apartment with such rage and anger that I feared he would unleash it on me physically. This was the first, but certainly not the last time, he would have me fearing for my physical well-being and even my life. I suffered from my first anxiety attack while I was seven months pregnant, as I was showering. I began screaming so uncontrollably that I thought I was going to die. I had never experienced not being in control of my own body. I literally could not stop screaming.

My body trembled excessively, and I began to hyperventilate, and the only thought that was running through my mind at the time was "Lord, I think I am losing it." The anxiety attack was following a very volatile argument that led to our entire apartment being destroyed yet again.

My husband, the man that I vowed I would love forever and vowed my life to, broke tables, glass, picture frames and managed to put a nice size hole in our bedroom door with his fist. He snatched clothes from our closet and had strewn them all over. He broke the television, along with the mirror to our dresser. As he tore through the house like a wild animal, he screamed and yelled and violated me verbally again and again, repeatedly calling me out of my name. His actions scared me, but more than that, his words scarred me. I immediately locked myself in our bathroom and called my sister. Even though she and I we were not in a very good place with one another, she was all I had, and so I turned to her. I was hysterical and in a state of panic and shock. Leah asked the basic questions about my safety and left it at that. While I don't believe she wanted me to get hurt, part of me believed that she felt I was getting what I deserved.

My life was again unravelling by the seams, and I felt I was not in control of the situation. Omari never knocked on the door, he never came to see about me, and he never asked what happened. Once the attack subsided, I wrapped myself in my robe and sat outside on the bare ground of our patio. I watched cars go by for hours and stared off into space. My body, my baby, and my mind were all in a state of shock, and I felt every last piece of it. As the calendar days of our marriage went by, the abuse continued. I longed for the reassuring words that I believe only my mother could have given me. Absent to me was the comfort of being able to turn to her in my time of worry and distress. The world can be a very cold and lonely place when a girl's mother is not in her life to guide her. I believe many of the changes and hardships I experienced in life would have never occurred if she was still had been alive to nurture me through fleeting thoughts and silly, misguided desires.

After a little over two years of sacrificing myself to the emotional, mental, financial and verbal abuse, I could no longer take what I was being given. To boot, Omari was a habitual cheater and liar. The last straw was his expressed desire to want to kill me with a knife that had been strategically placed under our mattress. He showed me the knife and where it was hidden, and from that point on, I lived in complete and total fear. I had begun to be stressed so heavily that I lost weight and was down to a sad and desolate looking 111 lbs., standing at 5'6". I had become a shell of a young woman, and my concern not only for my well-being but my daughter's as well was ever-pressing.

By the fall of 2002, I was so emotionally depleted I made the decision to pack up my baby and my belongings and leave Omari for good. I had made a few attempts in the past to leave but never stuck with them because of my desire to keep my family together. The desire to have completeness in place of the void that was created by my mother's death and my father's absence often superseded sound judgement and wisdom. I never wanted my daughter to grow up in a single-parent home. My greatest desire for her was to be loved and know it. Shattered dreams happen every day and for me, at that time, I felt as though I had been walking barefoot on those shatters since I was fifteen years old and was now creating them for my very own daughter.

Originally, I reached out to my sister for support. I asked her for six months or less stay in her home to get on my feet and find my own place, in order to escape the hell that I was in. She declined my ask; even though I was steadily employed and had never demonstrated a lack of progressiveness in my life. I remained a student even through the most turbulent of times; I worked, had a car and childcare, but still the answer was, no. More rejection, more abandonment, more frustration, more unforgiveness. In a time that I needed her the most, she was not there for me, forcing me to look other places. Thankfully, my sister's paternal brother allowed me and my baby to take residence in his home. I remained there from the end of November 2002 to the middle of February 2003. It was a total of 85 days…85 days that was given to me out of love, out of being considered family, even though we shared no blood and more than anything compassion. In that time, I did a tremendous amount of reflecting. Reflecting on who I could count on, reflecting on the poor choices I had made, and reflecting on how those choices could ultimately affect my future if I was not careful about my choices moving forward. During that time, Omari showed me who he was as a parent and that will forever be emblazoned in my mind. Once him and I were no longer together, he refused to see our daughter. He made empty promises to pick her up and removed himself completely from being financially responsible. Even though our daughter was young, she was still quite aware of the changes that had taken place and often questioned her father's whereabouts and for that I had no answer.

God saw fit for me to find a rental home in a neighboring south suburban community, and I decided to share space with my sister-in-law (Ryan's sister). That plan came together beautifully. We decided to rent the house together for one year and go our separate ways after that. In that year, I discovered some things about myself that I didn't know and started the healing process of what I had experienced during the course of my hazardous marriage and toxic relationship with Leah. Men were not my focus; neither was allowing Omari to mend our family back together again. I simply wanted to work, go to school, and take care of my baby, and for the most part that is what I did.

Towards the tail end of me and Omari living together, I began to delve into the club scene and frequented many clubs in Chicago's downtown area on the weekends. During this time, my childhood friends and I became close again and that closeness grew when he was completely out of the picture.

In my new place that I shared with my sister-in-law, they visited often when on break from school or whenever they decided to come home. We partied and lived the life of young women figuring out life with little to no worries. There were some mistakes made along that journey and many lessons learned; however, I was coming into my own as a woman but still sadly very much misguided without the presence of my mother. Most of what she taught me stayed with me and the basics I held very close to my heart, even until now. Nevertheless, there are some things that I just had to experience, despite the warning signs.

Do not forget the lessons taught, with every
day that we live apply them as needed—
Never forgetting that in those experiences, you
are being refined, renewed, and strengthened.

-Carsen Aminna

8

BEYOND THE BROKENNESS

Some five years passed, and I bore another child. I endured many hardships during the course of that pregnancy. Hardships that included homelessness, unemployment and abandonment. The father of my second born and I broke up rather early in the pregnancy and I found myself alone with not one but now two children to care for. My desire for things to go differently was present, but early on in my quest I still lacked the wisdom and proper self-love to choose a partner more wisely. Choosing a mate from a place of hurt, rejection, or plain old boredom most likely will result in drama and a sorrowful ending. Despite the trying times, I continued on with school and began creating a life for myself that I was proud of but still felt was incomplete. There were goals that I wanted to accomplish to make myself and my mother proud. There were places and things that I wanted my children to see and have; so, while I was in a good place in my life, I knew it could be better, and I fought for that better dream.

After living in years of marital purgatory, I made the move to finally file for a divorce from Omari in 2006 and officially, laid it all to rest. Even though him and I were both in relationships with other people and both had other children, I was truly done with him and the marriage itself; never revisiting any romantic endeavors, this was something that I felt needed to be done, so that I could make room for any blessings from God.

With a divorce under my belt and two children in tow, I earnestly began to seek God's face with my whole heart and search to fill the emptiness that a life without Him as my primary focus presented to me. In my complete brokenness and desire to be used by God, things in my life began to change. I stopped walking in the shadow of my mother's death and being overcome by the rejection and abandonment created by my father's absence along with friends and family's choices that seemed to plague me. I made an active choice to forgive my father, my ex-husband, and even Leah and Ryan. Though some offenses are harder to forgive than others and it becomes especially challenging when people repeat the same actions that hurt you in the first place, there is still opportunity for healing.

I have learned to set boundaries and expectations for people's actions to match their words. I have learned to listen to wisdom and to always seek God in all things, whether big or small in my life. I have also gathered that people will fail, and so much so, that it will exceed your understanding, but God is still a redeemer.

Learning that we cannot place expectations of what we would do, onto others, is a hard life lesson to learn, especially in the face of sickness, death, marriage, divorce, pregnancy, and any other life-altering situation that comes along. Accepting people for what and where they are is one thing, but deciding to leave them where they stand because what they give or don't give affects you is something altogether different. Womanhood is phenomenal and exciting, heart-breaking and trying, filled with promises and also failures. It is what you choose to make it.

If I could guess it, I would imagine that walking the road to womanhood is a ton easier with a mother to walk beside you. A mother to help bear the load, hold your hand, wipe your tears, and calm your fears. I would also imagine that having that unrelenting, always forgiving and always abounding type of love would steady a young girl's feet so well, that even when the tides of life come in to destroy her, and mistakes are made, she is sure that it will not overtake her. That kind of love builds confidence; it helps to build a trust within herself to choose her audiences wisely and that she is capable of handling life and handling it well.

For the motherless girl, who is now a woman, remember to reach back and give. Give what you so desperately needed as a girl to another girl that is without a mother. Contribute to help fulfilling a destiny, that might otherwise be unfulfilled. Reach out to aid in healing a bleeding heart and remember the familiarness of your pain; at all cost, do your best not to add to theirs.

Remember the miles you walked and the shoes you walked them in. Do not forget the prayers you prayed and the tears you cried for better nights and better days. Let your decisions to be sympathetic be ones that are driven by the heart and not the head, for the girl will know the difference. Be transparent about your mistakes, in turn easing the load of despair for when they make their own. Be loving, be patient, be kind, but most importantly, be YOUR most AUTHENTIC SELF.

To those who have never lost a mother, you too can be a light. Choose to be a village, instead of an island. Extend yourself beyond what you believe you are capable of, even if you think you are not able to; sometimes the reach is all a girl needs. As intangible as her pain maybe to you, the thread that you share, is being human; walk in your humanness alongside of her. Prayers are always beneficial and needed; checking in with a short text or a quick pop-up without being asked or prompted first, shows that you actually care. Doubting yourself and the capacity of which you can be of service to her is ineffective; we all are given a special set of talents or gifts, simply walking in those gifts and sharing them with her may be all that she needs to feel as though all is not lost. A little bit goes a long way, I promise.

Printed in the United States
By Bookmasters